T0081148

This or That

Questions
About
Technology

You Decide!

by Stephanie Bearce

CAPSTONE PRESS
a capstone imprint

Capstone Captivate is published by Capstone Press, an imprint of Capstone.
1710 Roe Crest Drive
North Mankato, Minnesota 56003
www.capstonepub.com

Library of Congress Cataloging-in-Publication Data
Names: Bearce, Stephanie, author.
Title: This or that questions about technology : you decide! / by Stephanie Bearce.
Description: North Mankato, Minnesota : Capstone Press, [2021] | Series: This or that?: science edition | Includes index. | Audience: Ages 8-11 | Audience: Grades 4-6 | Summary: "Technology is advancing rapidly. Transportation experts think self-driving cars could fill the streets someday soon. Designers are experimenting with different artificial intelligence devices. The choices designers make now will affect our future. What choices would you make in a world of new technology? Would you rather use nanobots or a wearable health monitor? Would you rather take to the skies with a jet pack or on a flying motorcycle? Would you rather have telescopic eyesight or supersonic hearing? It's your turn to pick this or that!"-- Provided by publisher.
Identifiers: LCCN 2020033472 (print) | LCCN 2020033473 (ebook) | ISBN 9781496695697 (hardcover) | ISBN 9781496696977 (paperback) | ISBN 9781977155122 (pdf) | ISBN 9781977156747 (kindle edition)
Subjects: LCSH: Technology--Miscellanea--Juvenile literature.
Classification: LCC T48 .B42 2021 (print) | LCC T48 (ebook) | DDC 600--dc23
LC record available at https://lccn.loc.gov/2020033472
LC ebook record available at https://lccn.loc.gov/2020033473

Image Credits
Getty Images: Michael Cole, 7; iStockphoto: janiecbros, 9, MATJAZ SLANIC, 16, Supersmario, 28; Newscom: JP5\ZOB\WENN.com, 26; Shutterstock: Andrey_Popov, 20, Chesky, 11, Evgeniyqw, 14, 17, goffkein.pro, 23, GoodStudio, design element, Gorodenkoff, 15, 22, happyphotons, 27, HQuality, 25, khoamartin, 3, Leone_V, design element, Margot Petrowski, 18, metamorworks, cover bottom right, 4–5, 10, NosorogUA, 24, Ollyy, 8, PaO_STUDIO, 29, Phonlamai Photo, cover bottom left, Pixsooz, 21, Rawpixel.com, 12, Titima Ongkantong, design element, tsuneomp, cover top left, 6, Volodymyr Horbovyy, 13, VTT Studio, 19

Editorial Credits
Editor: Carrie Sheely; Designer: Sarah Bennett; Media Researcher: Tracy Cummins; Production Specialist: Spencer Rosio

All internet sites appearing in back matter were available and accurate when this book was sent to press.

Words in **bold** are in the glossary.

Technology Today and Beyond

Radios, televisions, and computers were new **technologies** that changed the world. They made it easier for people to communicate and learn. They also provided new forms of entertainment.

Today, people are inventing new technologies faster than ever. They include 3-D printers, drones, robots, and more. Someday, people might ride in fully self-driving vehicles. Jet packs could become a popular way to travel through the air.

But using new technology isn't always perfect, and it can come with risks. Problems in a medical device can cause health risks. In self-driving vehicles, problems could cause crashes that harm people.

How to Use This Book

This book is full of questions that relate to technology and the future. The questions are followed by information to help you come to a decision. Pick one or the other. There are no wrong answers! But think carefully about your decisions because some could mean the difference between life and death. Are you ready? Turn the page to pick this or that!

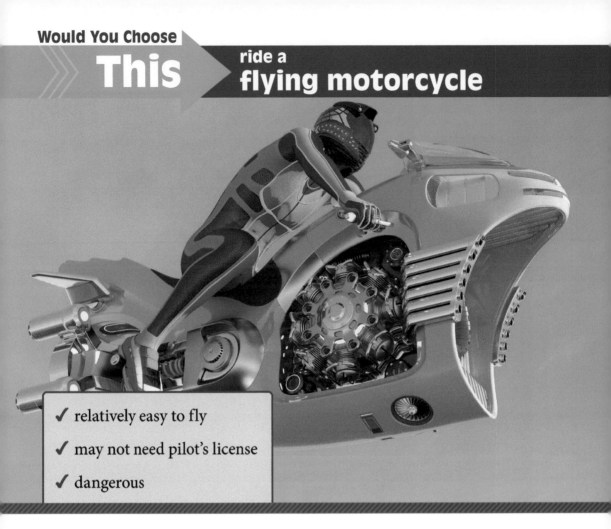

✔ relatively easy to fly

✔ may not need pilot's license

✔ dangerous

Imagine zipping across town on a flying motorcycle! These motorcycles have special equipment to keep them level in the air. This makes them easier to fly. Some can be flown without a pilot's license. But riding a flying motorcycle is dangerous. Some fly thousands of feet in the air. Crashes could be deadly.

OR
That?
fly with a
personal jet pack

- ✔ small size
- ✔ mostly for short trips
- ✔ need a lot of training

For years, scientists have been working on technology for jet packs. People strap jet packs onto their backs. The packs use small engines powered by jet fuel. Today, people can use them for only short trips. Operating a jet pack is not easy. A pilot must have hours of training. Like with other flying vehicles, crashes can be deadly.

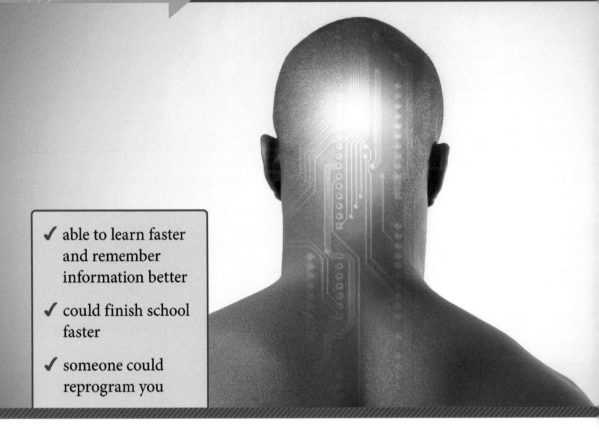

- ✓ able to learn faster and remember information better
- ✓ could finish school faster
- ✓ someone could reprogram you

The human nervous system is crackling with electricity. Scientists could use this electricity to power **microchips** in the brain. Microchips could send signals to connect the brain to a computer or **artificial intelligence** (AI) technology. This could increase a person's memory and rate of learning. You could whiz through school. But it is not totally safe. Someone could break into the network and reprogram your brain.

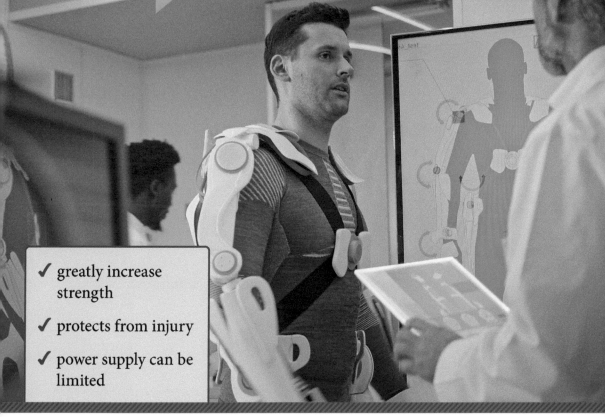

- ✓ greatly increase strength
- ✓ protects from injury
- ✓ power supply can be limited

Exoskeletons are metal frameworks fitted with motorized "muscles." People could wear them to increase their strength. Lifting 200 pounds (91 kilograms) would be easy. The skeletons shield bones and muscles to protect them from injury. But exoskeletons need a lot of power. Batteries would need to be recharged regularly.

✔ convenient

✔ can prevent crashes caused by distracted or sleepy drivers

✔ errors in the technology can cause crashes

Today, people are testing self-driving cars. But these cars have a human driver to take over if anything goes wrong. Experts think someday there will be cars that don't need human drivers. People can relax and let the cars' sensors and computers work. The cars can prevent crashes caused by distracted or sleepy drivers. But they won't be perfect, and errors could be deadly.

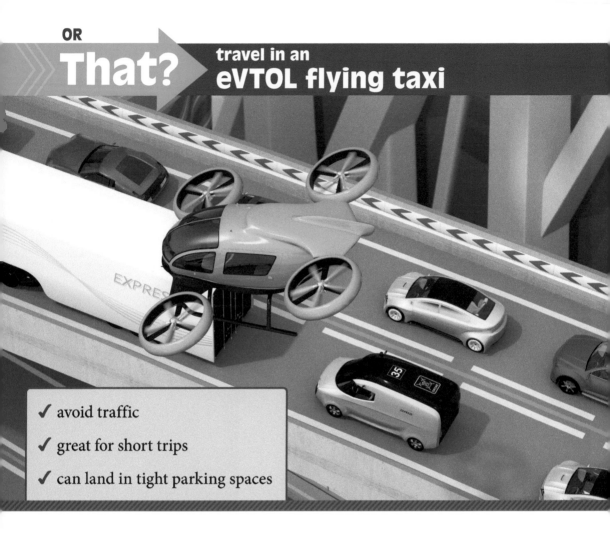

- ✓ avoid traffic
- ✓ great for short trips
- ✓ can land in tight parking spaces

Need to get across town in a hurry? Someday you might be able to call an eVTOL (electric vertical take-off and landing) air taxi to pick you up! These electric vehicles would soar above traffic jams. They take off and land vertically like helicopters. They can land in tight spaces. But they would only be for short trips.

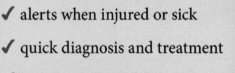

✔ alerts when injured or sick

✔ quick diagnosis and treatment

✔ could malfunction

Someday your clothes might keep you healthy. Clothes could be made with wires and sensors to turn them into health monitors. You could have a shirt that takes your temperature and checks your heart rate. The information could be sent to your doctor. The doctor could suggest medicines. But if it **malfunctions**, you could get treated for the wrong sickness. You could also get treated when there is nothing wrong. This can be risky to your health.

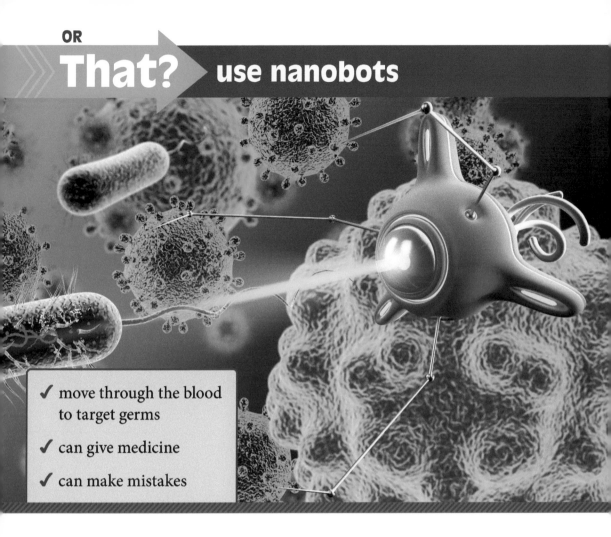

✔ move through the blood to target germs

✔ can give medicine

✔ can make mistakes

Nanobots are tiny machines that can be put into the human body. They move through the bloodstream to find sick **cells**. They hunt down germs and kill them. Nanobots can also give medicine. Using nanobots can be risky. They might treat the wrong cells or give the wrong medicine.

✓ travel back and forth from Earth to space stations

✓ a lot of responsibility

✓ dangerous job

Space pilots blast into space at speeds of more than 17,000 miles (28,000 kilometers) per hour. They move people and supplies from Earth to space stations such as the International Space Station (ISS). Being a space pilot takes a great deal of training. Space pilots are responsible for the safety of the spacecraft and crew. They must know how to fix equipment. Equipment problems in space can be deadly.

✔ growing career

✔ design how robots look

✔ deal with customer complaints

Robot designers work in a growing career. People use robots in factories, homes, and hospitals. To be robot designers, people usually go to college for at least four years. Robot designers decide how robots will look, work, and communicate. They design sensors for the robots. Robot designers need to be good problem solvers. If customers have problems, designers need to fix them quickly.

✓ see unique underwater creatures

✓ in small space

✓ dangerous

Want to see blobfish? You might if you took a trip on a submersible! These small submarines can go thousands of feet below the ocean's surface. Deep-sea tourists can watch amazing animals such as octopuses and sea turtles. But the trips are dangerous. There's always the risk of leaks. The farther a sub goes down, the more the weight of the water above presses on it. The sub can be crushed if it breaks.

✓ dangerous

✓ very expensive

✓ get to see outer space

Want to be a space tourist? A ride to outer space can cost more than $200,000. But space tourists get the experience of a lifetime. They experience **weightlessness** as they float in spaceships and get amazing views. The trips are risky. Broken equipment and crashes can easily become deadly.

- ✓ always available to talk
- ✓ need power to work
- ✓ not a real friendship

Need a best friend who is always there? Artificial intelligence best friends never need to sleep. The only job of an AI friend is to talk to its human. Through AI, they learn about their human friends over time. AI friends can help people feel less lonely. But they can't go on adventures with you. And they don't work without batteries or electricity. They also might need an internet connection.

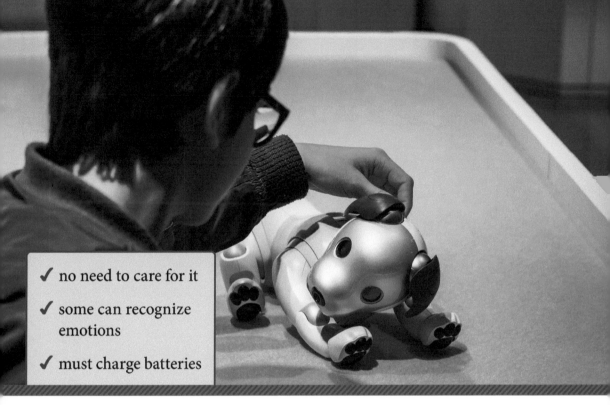

✓ no need to care for it

✓ some can recognize emotions

✓ must charge batteries

Robot cats are cuddly. Some robot dogs can be trained to do tricks. Robot pets don't need to go to the vet or get baths. You don't need to clean up their poop or pee. Some can learn to understand and respond to your emotions. They do require batteries, and like anything mechanical, they can break down.

✔ able to see great distances

✔ can use to spy

✔ can only be worn a short time

Imagine seeing objects clearly from a mile away with just a blink! Inventors are testing contact lenses with **telescopic** sight. They use light bouncing off tiny aluminum mirrors. The lenses can make objects appear almost three times larger than they really are. Today, it's only safe to wear the lenses a short time. Scientists are working to increase the wearing time.

✓ able to pick up very soft sounds

✓ able to hear danger before it arrives

✓ might be able to hear noises outside human range of hearing

Scientists have been developing earbuds to give soldiers super hearing. The earbuds make loud noises softer. Gunfire and other loud sounds then won't damage a soldier's hearing. The earbuds also can pick up very soft noises and make them louder. They could help soldiers hear enemies nearby and save lives. Future technology could help people hear sounds outside the human **range** of hearing.

- ✓ 3-D images help you see what objects really look like
- ✓ can share ideas with people without traveling
- ✓ need expensive computer and headgear

Holographic computers can let you see the world without leaving home! They use light to **project** 3-D images. Using these computers, you could walk around and see objects. You just couldn't touch them because they are only light. Inventors can send 3-D images of inventions to people around the world. They can make changes to inventions without traveling. But the computers and the headgear are expensive. One system costs around $50,000.

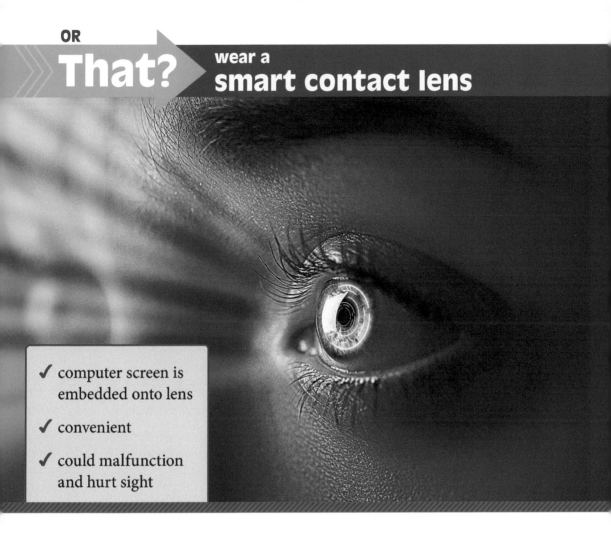

That? wear a smart contact lens

- ✓ computer screen is embedded onto lens
- ✓ convenient
- ✓ could malfunction and hurt sight

Want to get information with a quick glance? You might be able to soon. Scientists are developing a smart contact lens with an embedded computer screen. With it, you wouldn't need to wear glasses or headsets. You could control the lens with eye movements and gestures. You could check the forecast, see your calendar, and get other information. But a lens with electronics in your eye can be risky. If it malfunctions, your eye could be damaged.

✔ need only food ingredients and a 3-D printer

✔ makes mealworms and other insects look more appetizing

✔ might help solve hunger problems

Hungry? Just print yourself a snack. A 3-D printer can print materials in layers. The printer can use pureed food, mealworm paste, or even seaweed to print food. Some people don't like the way seaweed or mealworm paste looks. But if it's printed like a pizza or a hamburger, they might want to eat it. Ingredients such as insects are widely available. Using them could help reduce world hunger.

✔ no animals are killed

✔ more friendly to the environment than regular meat processing

✔ texture can be different from real meat

Scientists have invented a new way to grow meat. The cells of a chicken or cow are placed in a dish. The cells are fed a chemical mix of proteins and amino acids. The cells grow and multiply to make meat strips. The meat is harvested. It can be made into different shapes. No animals are killed to make this meat. Because meat grows in a lab, the process is more friendly to the **environment**. But some people say the texture can be different from animal meat.

✓ help save lives of military members

✓ could sneak around enemy land

✓ can hide from targeting systems

Technology for militaries can be a matter of life and death for soldiers. For years, militaries have been making vehicles that are hard for enemies to find or see. Companies have developed technology to hide huge vehicles such as tanks from **infrared** targeting equipment. One system can make a tank look like its surroundings. It can also make the tank look like cars, rocks, or other objects.

✓ able to sneak around anywhere

✓ hide and fool people

✓ others can use one too

Ever dreamed of having an invisibility cloak? It sounds like magic, but it's technology. One company has made a material that bends light. This hides any object under the material. Scientists are using the material in experiments with militaries. Someday this material or one like it may be available to the public. With an invisibility cloak, you could pull tricks on friends. But your friends could use a cloak to fool you too!

✓ fresh food available

✓ get health benefits of vegetables

✓ need to check that plants are growing properly

Need some fresh herbs for your pizza? Just open the refrigerator! Some refrigerators have grow lights and devices that control the temperature to grow vegetable plants. The plants grow in water with nutrients in it. But you would still need to check on the plants. And the fridge wouldn't work without electricity.

- ✓ fewer kitchen chores
- ✓ try new recipes
- ✓ adjust diet to each person's needs

Cooking could be super simple with a robot chef to do the cutting, stirring, cooking, and cleaning. A robot chef could be programmed to adjust food to each person's dietary needs. Allergic to peanuts or wheat? The robot chef would avoid those ingredients. Tired of the same recipes? You could program the robot to whip up something new.

Lightning Round
Would you choose to . . .

➡ ride in a hover car that floats just above roads
or on a maglev train that hovers above train tracks?

➡ have a closet that cleans your clothes
or a robot that brings snacks?

➡ invent a boat that helps clean the ocean
or an airplane that helps clean the air?

➡ have a robot teacher
or an online classroom?

➡ have a sweat-powered smartwatch
or air-conditioned clothes?

➡ use artificial intelligence to spy
or to block others from spying?

➡ use facial recognition computer programs
or eye recognition computer programs?

➡ have a flying car that travels on roads and in the air
or have a personal air vehicle that only flies?

Glossary

artificial intelligence (ar-ti-FISH-uhl in-TEL-uh-junss)—capability of a machine to imitate intelligent human behavior

cell (SEL)—a basic part of an animal or plant that is so small you can't see it without a microscope

environment (in-VY-ruhn-muhnt)—the natural world of the land, water, and air

exoskeleton (ek-soh-SKE-luh-tuhn)—a man-made outer supporting structure that people can wear

infrared (in-fruh-RED)—a type of light that is invisible to human eyes; infrared cameras can detect objects by the heat they give off

malfunction (mal-FUHNGK-shun)—to fail to work correctly

microchip (MYE-kroh-chip)—a tiny circuit that processes information in a computer

nanobot (NA-no-bot)—a very small robot

project (PROH-ject)—to cause light to fall on a surface

range (RAYNJ)—the difference between the least and greatest values of something, such as the range of hearing

technology (tek-NOL-uh-jee)—the use of science to do practical things, such as designing complex machines

telescopic (te-luh-SKAH-pik)—suitable for seeing or magnifying distant objects

weightlessness (WAYT-luhs-nes)—lacking apparent gravitational pull

Read More

Amin, Anita Nahta. *What Would It Take to Make a Jet Pack?* North Mankato, MN: Capstone Press, 2020.

Klepeis, Alicia Z. *The Future of Transportation: From Electric Cars to Jet Packs.* North Mankato, MN: Capstone Press, 2020.

Swanson, Jennifer. *National Geographic Kids: Everything Robotics: All the Robotic Photos, Facts, and Fun!* Washington, D.C.: National Geographic, 2016.

Internet Sites

Easy Science for Kids: All About Robotics
easyscienceforkids.com/all-about-robotics/

Kiddle: Technology Facts for Kids
kids.kiddle.co/Technology

Time for Kids: Sky Rides
www.timeforkids.com/g56/sky-rides/